T0162569

Author's note:

A legacy of funny stuff, whimsical, sentimental, sardonic, even erudite stuff. I like the funny stuff best.

Thanks to:
Helen, my beautiful wife and illustrator
Max Morath, my urger-in-chief
Ian Sharkey of Apple, who sent it all into space

After long years in advertiting, Ed and Helen Caffrey live on a lovely farm in New Jersey.
She's a psychotherapist and he teaches Italian to adults.

(About the poem "50 Words Will Shortz Can't Do Without"):
"Excellent! This belongs in print!"
—Billy Collins, former U.S. Poet Laureate

ACCESSIBLE VERSES
HUMOR IN POETRY

ED CAFFREY

iUniverse, Inc.
Bloomington

Accessible Verses
Humor in Poetry

iUniverse books may be ordered through booksellers or by contacting:

iUniverse
1663 Liberty Drive
Bloomington, IN 47403
www.iuniverse.com
1-800-Authors (1-800-288-4677)

ISBN: 978-1-4620-3217-4 (sc)
ISBN: 978-1-4620-3218-1 (ebk)

Printed in the United States of America

iUniverse rev. date: 08/01/2011

ACCESSIBLE VERSES

No days but these,
no Praesidium but this,
no silence but my own.
Drift of dead mind
In mind, noon its own spectre.
                              -Matthew Mead

Enigmatic to read is our Mister Mead,
while mine is accessible verse,
insufficiently mystic or ambiguistic,
hermetical, arcane or terse.
He receives checks while I get rejects
from poetry journals, so while
I mull the blatantly sordid inequity,
just sit back and read 'em and smile.

WANDERLUST

I sat in my rowboat and stared straight up
at that leviathan rotund stern.
WANDERLUST, BALDWIN N.Y. it read,
and it made my fantasy churn.
Wanderlust, Wanderlust, what did it mean,
I wondered, naively, at ten.
I asked my mother, who fumfered on "lust",
but "urge to roam" did it for then.
Urge to roam, urge to roam, what did that mean?
Beyond Baldwin and straight out to sea?
Could it be possible that this big-rump tub
might cast off her lines and break free?
I saw her in Bali, Tahiti, Siam,
native girls in the lagoon,
over to Hong Kong, trading in spices,
then around Bombay to Rangoon.
The South Atlantic, African side,
chug chugging past Senegal,
around to Egypt and up the Nile,
from the Baldwin to the Suez Canal.
But then, somewhat later, to my boyish chagrin,
I learned the truth, painfully stark:
The Wanderlust never had been to Rangoon,
not even to Asbury Park.

She seldom if ever chugged out beyond
a half mile or so offshore,
from Montauk to Rockaway, skimming up clams
from the Long Island littoral floor.
That made her just a voluminous version
of my little boat there at the pier.
She went out clamming five days a week,
me maybe three times a year.
But I wondered if the Captain, as he fired her up,
ever turned to his crew and said,
"I tell you what, boys, now what do you say,
we forget about clams and instead
we head her south, south southeast,
say goodbye to the Baldwin Creek,
and we sail her to Bimini or Grand Bahama,
we can be there in less than a week."
Not at all likely, a silly idea
of a dreamy-eyed ten-year-old kid.
The Wanderlust never did get far from Baldwin,
but the kid in the rowboat did.

With thanks to Fred Stenzel.

THE IRISH HEALTH PLAN, 1945

Unerring thermometer, Mom's hand on my head.
102? Hot lemonade and blankets. Sleep.
Next morning, still 102. Tea and toast (Silvercup).
That evening, still 102. Hot toddy, milk and whiskey.
12 years old: me, not it.
Pile on the blankets, add a rug.
Sweat it out.
Next morning I'm cured or dead,
more than likely cured.

ANYTING F'TANKSGIVIN?

About nine in the morning we were ready to go,
the Ragamuffin Brigade,
a tattered troop of little hobos,
ceremoniously arrayed
in rags. Well, correction: in clothes that we'd worn
up to a month before,
that our mothers had saved for this last occasion,
then used to wipe up the floor.
We in the Harbor were not that far
from actual ragamuffinism,
living as we did each day of our lives
six feet from the dark abysm.
The kids uptown , for Thanksgiving Day,
to go begging door to door,
had to ask their moms to get them some rags
from a costume rental store.
So off we went, knock knock knock,
"Anyting f'Tanksgivin please?"
in our Long Island accents, not all that far
from genuine Brooklynese.
The people we called on were as bad off as we,
but they knew we were coming so when
we knocked there were marshmallows, pennies and apples,
all gone by a quarter past ten.
Trick or treating on Halloween
was a generation away.
When I was ten, all of us kids
bagged our loot on Thanksgiving Day.

A YANKEE GAME WITH SUSIE, 1948

Eddie Caffrey and Susie Hartmann,
exotics in a redneck town.
Catholic boy and Jewish girl,
peckerwoods all around.
Good friends we were, but more than that,
a date when we wanted a date.
Those North Baldwin girls were a snooty bunch,
but Sue was my Harbor soulmate.
One Sunday morning we got on the train
to Penn Station and onto the D.
One-Sixty-First Street, Bronx, New York,
down the walkway, around to Gate C,
up the ramp and there was the field,
an Eden of emerald green,
a memory stamped in indelible ink
to two boonie kids of fifteen.
Yanks and Athletics, one seventy-five,
plus a program, a life souvenir,
add hot dogs and Cokes, it came to eight bucks.
Today that's the price of a beer.
Mel Allen was the Yankees' radio voice,
the maestro of play-by-play.
Bob Shepard gave the lineups with class and restraint
on the sound-rebounding Stadium P.A.

Leading off at short was my fave, Phil Rizzuto,
the reason I always wore #10.
Batting second, playing second, #1, Snuffy Stirnweiss,
Tommy Henrich batted third, and then,
"Batting fourth, playing center, the Yankee Clipper,
#5, Joe DiMaggio-o-o..."
A lovely memory of an August day,
sixty-one years ago.
Even fonder is my memory of Susie Hartmann,
my first-grade through high schoolmate,
My chum, my buddy, my amiga, my pal,
and occasionally, my date.

With special thanks to Jack Lauhoff.

DOUBLE FEATURE AT THE BALDWIN
MOVIE THEATER, 1944

I got there when I got there,
let's say ten of six or so,
and I slid my way in, excuse me,
to the middle of the row.
Ann Sheridan was smiling
in the arms of Errol Flynn,
cooing "Will you be my man?",
on the verge of mortal sin.
Then THE END and all those credits,
the produced, directed bys.
Then the newsreel, and what news!
The U.S. with our allies
were mopping up the remnants
of a lightning-swift advance,
all those broken supermen,
kaput in Central France.
Next a short, a Pete Smith dilly
or a Lou Lehr monkeyshine,
and then the second feature,
"Bride of Frankenstein".
Then the Warner Brothers' logo,
and pretty soon there's Ann,
ah Ann, my gorgeous Ann,
cooing "Will you be my man?"
And I thought, beyond my years,
oh, if I were only Flynn,
and I slid my way out, excuse me,
saying "Here's where I came in."

1935

The penny postcard was,
and the three-cent stamp.
Campbell's Soup cost eight cents,
Ivory Soap nine.
A gallon of Shell was nineteen cents,
a Ford to burn it $495.
The leading box office actress, seven years old,
starred in four films.
Fred Astaire danced cheek to cheek,
while Cole Porter began the beguine.
Huey Long, Ma Barker and Dutch Schultz bought it.
Mussolini raped Ethiopia
and the Shah turned Persia to Iran.
Babe Ruth retired while Ella and Billie debuted,
along with Fibber McGee, Dick Tracy, Flash Gordon,
Your Hit Parade, social security, radar,
night baseball and the Douglas DC-3.
My writing career was progressing apace;
I could make a pretty good E.

ICE AND FIRE

July

In the morning a truck pulls up outside.
The door reads Joseph Beato and Sons.
Apelike young Louie knocks. How big?
Fifty cents, she says. That's an icebox filler.
Burlap on shoulder, icecake on burlap,
he sings: I only have ice for you!
It's gone in three days, dripping rusty into a pan.

November

In the morning a truck backs into the driveway.
Joseph Beato and Sons. Louie rigs his chutes,
yanks a lever and two tons of Kentucky blue coal
crash into the bin, louder than D-Day.

March

Fireman boots on, she splashes across the cellar floor,
shovels wet Kentucky blue on the banked amber glow,
a furnace as big as Titanic's, scarcely fifty degrees upstairs.
She shakes down ashes, shovels them wet into a heavy can,
wrestles it up four steps and out.
She does; he's never home and I'm too little.

May

No more fire, so no hot water.
Heat up a kettle, sponge wash in the sink.
No shower, ever, no fixture for one.
Young Lincoln would have felt at home.

eight years later

Fifteen, I bus to my aunt's
new apartment in Parkchester.
She offers a Coke from a Frigidaire
that makes, not takes, ice.
In the bathroom, tile and chrome,
like a Caddy with the key in the ignition, there it is.
May I? Of course, take your time.
My first shower alone, no boys waiting with towels.
Unworried about using all the hot,
in cascading jubiliation I vow:
I will earn ten thousand dollars in one year,
one day.

BALDWIN HARBOR, 1940

The soft southern breeze was redolent of swamp,
that vast cattail mile of muck,
from the last shack down to the Great South Bay.
It carried cinderbits from the garbage fires
along the bog road
and kerosene from the creekside hovel stoves.
The breezes east and west brought a fetid waft
of defunct sealife washed up the creeks from the bay.
The northern breeze bore a whiff of Republican comfort
from our uptown townsmen.
Then on a day in July the tar trucks came,
asperging bituminous gunk
on the roads and roadside grass,
followed by gravel spreaders and the dreadnought rollers.
Tar on our tires, tar on our soles,
tar in our noses day and night.
A week, a month, a summer.
Then a galeforce autumn southwind
blew it all north and dropped swampy cinderbits
onto roomier houses.

AMERICAN PHARMACOPEIA, 1940

Every kid got mumps.
Silent bedroom; noise=permanent hearing damage.
And measles. Worse, German measles.
A green shade; light=permanent eye damage.
And chicken pox.
Don't scratch, or the pock marks are permanent.
We'd learn in later years it was the setup for shingles.
We had few cures. No Salk, no penicillin,
no antibiotics at all.
But we had preventatives.
Every April every mother spring-cleaned the house
and spring-cleaned-out the kids.
Lore had it that frigid sunless winter
clogged passages, nasal and evacuative.
A purgative was required, the sterner the better.
Castor Oil, cathartic, Castoria, physic,
cod liver oil, ick.
Fleischmann's Yeast expels body poisons!
Your whole system is purified!
It was probably pure caca,
but yet, a lot of us are still here.

THE TENDEREST MEALS EVER, NO NUTRIENTS LOST!

-pressure cooker ad, 1948

"Famous Irish Chefs", it's been said,
is the slimmest book on the shelf.
We Irish are among the world's feebler cooks,
and that would include myself.
I'll chalk it up to the Famine, when we
had no bread, let alone gingerbread.
It's hard to master haute cuisine
when your crops are lying there dead.
But the blight receded, potatoes returned,
they're our specialty, as you may know.
We boil the nutrients out of the spuds,
and down the drain they go.
My grandmother Kate arrived from Ireland
in 1892.
She'd a recipe for mashed potatoes
and another for Irish stew.
She taught her daughter, my mother Kate,
those two and not much more.
But my dear Mom, an inventive lass,
sought other cuisines to explore.
Italian pasta, Mexican salsa,
I commend her, she gave it a go.
But Irish chili, Irish spaghetti?
Excuse me, you don't want to know.
Stew and potatoes were staples for us,
but the beef was always tough.
So I said to myself, at 15 or so,
enough, enough, enough..

I bought her a pressure cooker on sale
for eleven ninety-nine.
Come on, I delivered Newsdays then,
too poor for top-of-the-line.
But the beef in those first stews she made?
Soft outside, softer still underneath.
So soft was this heretofore rock-hard meat
that you needn't any teeth.
But then one day... I suppose it's true
that if I had paid more for the pot,
it would not have exploded the way it did
when it got a trifle too hot.
The top blew off, the stew went splat!
all over the ceiling and wall;
potatoes, tomatoes and tender beef,
hanging there, starting to fall.
I helped her clean up, my sweet darling Mom.
She said "It wasn't your fault, Eddie."
But the very next day we were back to a menu
of hot dogs and Irish spaghetti.

WHY THE YANKEES WON ALL THOSE PENNANTS

My front stoop, Saturday afternoon,
folding Newsdays to lob on 101 other stoops,
while reading Billy Rose and Jimmy Cannon
and listening to Mel Allen on my Emerson portable,
maroon plastic, the size of the O.E.D.,
the battery the size and weight of a brick.
Winter nights it terrified me with Inner Sanctum and Escape.
Not today. Today, baseball.
Yanks and Sox tied, top of the 8th. Decisive moment.
I set out on my bike, a gaudily gorgeous maroon Schwinn,
horn button, rear rack, a treasure,
finagled somehow through my Tammany uncle
by my grandmother for Christmas 1946,
when a new Schwinn could not be had.
Now its basket holds 101 Newsdays and Mel in the Emerson.
Rizzuto on second, Henrich up, two out.
If, and I firmly believe in that if,
if I sail one onto Brunner's stoop,
Henrich will drive him in.
If I miss, 3 out.
The moment: I fling... up, up, smack, flat on the top step.
Rizzuto scores easily.

EARLY CAREER CHANGE

When I was a teen in the forties,
a question occurred to me.
I was already half grown up,
so, decision: What did I want to be?
My early first choice was cowboy,
ridin' high out there in the west.
All other choices, like pilot,
were tied for a weak second best.
I'd be the new young Autry or Rogers,
it was pretty much settled til when
I listened close to the lyrics
of "Back in the Saddle Again":
>   Ridin' the range once more,
>   totin' my old 44,
>   where you sleep out every night
>   and the only law is right...
You sleep out every night?
In the snow and the sleet and the rain?
Downwind from a hundred cows
filling the air with methane?
No bed, no pillow, no mattress?
No woman? (Even then I knew.)
No thanks. So, a whole new decision:
What else would I like to do?
But I didn't rush the process,
it was a matter for more than a minute.
Just make it a job that includes a bed,
with a nice warm woman in it.

THE GOOD NEWS

On Church Street, a haberdasher;
polo shirts, dungarees, socks.
For workers, work socks with reinforced toes.
For bobbysoxers, bobby socks--
white for brown loafers,
a penny in the pouch, for show-offs a dime.
Costly socks, $5 a pair in now money.
And frail. After 5 washes, threadbare heel and toe.
Mothers sat listening to Blondie, darning.
Insert the egg, thread the needle,
make a weave, warp and woof.
Socks today? $8 for 6 pairs at Costco.
And tough. No eggs or needles needed.
There's a hole in the ozone,
the oceans are poisoned,
we're trillions in debt,
but socks
are better than ever.

SHELF LIFE

Hey!
It's me, up here,
top shelf, third from the left, red jacket.
Remember me?
You bought me, read me twice, said you loved me,
said I was so exciting you couldn't put me down.
So you put me up, top shelf, third from the left.
That was 23 years ago.
23 years, no other lovers.
I could have had dozens.
Should have, still could.
I'm as exciting as I was then,
still got all my pages, no coffee stains.
So what do you say?
Pass me on to someone you love,
to someone you like,
to just about anybody, but,
whomever it is, do mention my wanderlust.
I can do a new lover every month.

IL TEATRO ITALIANO

Italia, land of 60 million actors,
their operatic gestures embedded in childhood.
Anger: bite index finger knuckle, fume.
Delicious: turn index finger in cheek, blow kiss.
Don't give a damn: four-finger upswipe to chin, glower.
These are the theatrics that British drama schools
endeavor to teach,
that Italian drama schools endeavor to unteach,
and embed instead that less is more.
Anger: frown, clench jaw briefly.
Delicious: raise eyebrows, nod slightly.
Don't give a damn: short sneer, expel breath.
Italia, land of 60 million actors,
all brilliant, except for a few,
who are, of course, on stage.

A LONG OVERDUE THANK-YOU TO DICK TRACY

When I was a young lad, ten or so,
I read the comics with zeal:
Superman, Brenda Starr,
Invisible Scarlett O'Neill.
Dick Tracy each week provided a tip
in the on-going war against crime.
One stood out, a hard and fast rule
that still stands the test of time.
The cagiest felon, elusive and smooth,
a master of every ruse,
can be spotted and nabbed by the simple observance
of how he puts on his shoes.
Left one first? That means he's left-handed,
like that prison-break escapee.
And I thought, hmm, what if someday
the police come searching for me?
They'll be on the lookout for someone
who ties his right shoe first.
So I set out with serious purpose
to get that habit reversed.
I practiced and got it down perfect,
left foot first so as not to betray
my identity-- one of the reasons
I remain a free man today.

2 WAY
WRIST
RADIO

WEDNESDAY

I do the puzzle,
I let out the cat.
I walk the doggie
and after that,
I do my Italian,
take the pup for a poop,
then heat up a can
of Progresso soup,
take a walk, read my book,
then I let in the cat,
read the mail, pet the dog
and realize that
this day, this morning and afternoon
would be all that there is
to every day of every week
if my Helen weren't coming home soon.

VICKS VAPORUB

Your bedroom door opens.
Mom comes in softly and sits on the edge of your bed,
where you lie rasping with a head full of congestion.
She opens a small blue jar, undoes your jama top,
rubs the wonder lotion gently onto your chest,
then covers it with a towel warm from the oven.
You breathe in the healing haze with a sigh of solace...
and you sleep.
In 1880 a Carolina druggist mixed camphor,
an Asian wonderanalgesic,
also used in embalming and mothballs,
with eucalyptol, menthol and turpentine,
and sold it as VapoRub, effective in the relief of
nasal congestion, muscle soreness, coughing,
insect bites and bruises.
MayoClinic.com declares it virtually useless medically,
but that is not the point;
the active ingredient in Vicks VapoRub is nostalgia.

THIS I KNOW

I know who played and sang "Tico Tico",
George Stirnweiss's nickname,
who was Lincoln's first vice president,
the capital of Moldova,
all the words to "A You're Adorable",
Burt Lancaster's name in "The Train",
the coin of Haiti,
whom someone's in the kitchen with,
why the Model A came after the Model T,
the original Pepsi-Cola jingle,
Howdy Doody's manipulator,
Henry Aldrich's best friend,
Fred Astaire's real name,
Harry Truman's middle name,
how to say fart in French,
Joe DiMaggio's other brother,
all the words to "16 Tons",
what fongool means,
Jack Benny's announcer,
Kingfish's wife's name,
Milton Berle's Texaco men's song,

Who Snooky Lanson was,
Who first sang "Here she is, Miss America",
Dorothy's last name,
why Yankee Doodle called it macaroni,
if fish sleep,
the smallest country,
what a roman à clef is,
which movie won the most Oscars,
Lucy's and Linus's last name
and all 7 dwarfs and deadly sins.
And you know what?
All of that, combined and doubled,
is not worth a French fart.

SCENES ALONG THE JONES BEACH CAUSEWAY, 1941

Family with a flat.
Mom, Gram, kids sitting in the grass,
as sweating, blaspheming Dad
pumps the jack.

Two teen boys with towels around their necks,
hopeful thumbs pointing south.
Look, here comes a car...
please let it be two girls.

Model A boiling over.
Family in the car waits,
Dad with a rag turns the cap.
He tries to remember...
did he refill the water can?
Oh well, if not, once again,
wee-wee will have to do.

ADVICE TO SOMEONE REACHING 75

No more ladders.
Two rungs tops.
Anything higher, hire a boy.
No shoveling snow.
Same boy.
Don't swim in the ocean.
Don't even stand in the ocean.
Sit in the ocean.
No more fried food.
Mushy food now.
Kraft Dinner.
Stay over to the right.
Let them zoom by.
You're way, way ahead.

AND THE WINNER IS...

Joe Smith, the very first Mormon,
could not wait to go to bed.
He knew he'd wake up in the morning
with a vision from God in his head.
God told him to dig in a hillside,
he'd come up with three plates of gold,
inscribed in "Reformed Egyptian",
countless thousands years old.
They only needed translation,
and Joe was God's chosen guy.
No one else was to see them,
that was the word from on high.
They revealed that American Indians,
all those Otoes, Apaches and Crows,
are descendants of a lost tribe of Israel,
as every Mormon now knows.
They crossed over in boats of balsa
(We have Joe's divine guarantee)
and they settled someplace in Missouri,
in about, oh, 600 B.C.
Yes, I know what you're going to tell me,
there's this bridge you want me to buy,
but it's with extreme admiration
and utmost esteem that I,
noting there are 6 million Mormons,
tell you that Joe Smith stands tall,
above all the Doyles, Danes and Bernbachs,
as the greatest adman of all.

WAITRESS LEAVES DINNER BILL FOR FOUR WOMEN, $180.76

Kim slips a calculator out of her purse,
totes it all up, says to Kate
"That's forty-two dollars and fifteen cents."
And to Ann, "Forty-three twenty-eight."
To Margaret, "Let's see, you had the sole,
so for you, forty-nine eighty-three.
And I had the chocolate tiramisù,
so it's forty-five fifty for me."

WAITRESS LEAVES DINNER BILL
FOR FOUR MEN, $180.76

Every guy throws in three twenties,
saying "Kevin, is that about right?"
He says "What the hell, keep it all, honey",
and the four walk away in the night.

I've been there, and it's my testimony,
though my wife says it's low-grade bolony.

THE VINTNER OF NAZARETH

In the small rural village of Cana
in northcentral Galilee,
a debut was made two millenia past
that still divides you from me.
Jesus was there with His faithful twelve,
His Mom and His stepfather Joe.
When someone whispered in Mary's ear
that the wine was running low,
she turned and said Son, they have no wine,
or, in other words, make them some.
He said to her Mother, with all due respect,
my hour has not yet come.
She must have watched Him do marvels at home,
maybe lighting a flame with a nod,
and she knew He was waiting for just the moment
to reveal Himself as God.
He told the stewards to take six stone jars
and fill them all up from the well.
Then when the chief took a taste of the water,
the cup in his hand nearly fell.
The water was wine, and not Manischewitz,
but premier grand cru Chardonnay,
enough for ten weddings, five hundred plus liters,
that's four hundred bottles today.
So I'd like to ask you, you who condemn
drinking wine as sinful behavior,
maybe so, maybe not, but if it is,
just what does that make the Savior?

NEVER

I'll never see Michel Monnin again,
never have any reason to mention his name,
though he was important to us back then.
Nor Bill Camaratta, not that I'd want to,
but the finality of it is daunting, that never.
Helen says You never know, but I know: It's never.
If she's right and one day he's standing in front of me
in an airport ticket line and he turns around,
what will I say?
"Hello again, Bill, I never really liked you"?
No, we'd be obliged into a litany of "How's she?"
and "Have you spoken with him lately?" Agony.
Not to worry, it will never happen.
High school classes hold reunions to hold it off,
and that works, for a year.
Seventy-year-old faces with eighteen-year-old names,
your friend from English class in his grandfather's body.
Then: "Do you have a date for Saturday?"
Now: "What Medicare plan are you on?"
Even so, it's only a hundred or so,
of your thousands of school faces, work faces,
neighbors and relations.
Cousin Joan, Cousin Eileen, not a call in twenty years.
Gone. And yet I have their phone numbers.
I don't call because I don't have to.
At school, at work, with neighbors, family, I had to.
They were there, at the next desk, the next house.
Now I'm here, with a beautiful wife, a warm dog,
the latest Sopranos DVD...
I can't possibly call Cousin Joan today.

RUDY, LAPCAT DELUXE

Let me describe him: He's beautifully soft,
like a furry Blackglama mink stole.
His eyes are the color of molten gold,
his coat is the color of coal.
When he lies in your lap it is blissful indeed,
and most soporific as well.
If you were planning a venture, sit back and forget it;
you're going to be there for a spell.
Just think:
Patton would never have shelled a tank,
Clyde would never have robbed a bank,
Nathan would never have sold a frank
with Rudy on their laps.
Caesar would never have conquered Gaul,
Humpty would never have had a great fall,
Cinderella would never have gone to the ball
with Rudy on their laps.
Ahab would never have speared a whale,
Salome would never have shed a veil,
Wilde would never have gone to gaol
with Rudy on their laps.
Now we're here on the couch, his head on my thigh;
I daren't do anything rash.
Which is why, you'll agree, it's impossible for me
to get up and take out the trash.

PLAYGROUND POETRY

From the girls' side:

> Strawberry shortcake, cream on top,
> spell me the name of your sweetheart...
> A... B... C... D... E...
>
> A, my name is Alice and my husband's name is Al.
> We live in Alabama and we sell apples...
>
> I'll never go to Macy's any more, more, more.
> There's a big fat policeman at the door, door, door.
> Oh, he'll take you by the collar
> and he'll make you pay a dollar.
> Oh, I'll never go to Macy's any more, more, more.

From the boys' side:

> Up the river, down the lake,
> pitcher's got a bellyache.

Clearly, the muse of lyric poetry
favored the girls' side.

Thanks to Louise Matarazzo.

THE MAN ON THE CAN

Ettore Boiardi, accent on the AR,
sailed from Italia to follow his star.
It led him to Manhattan, where he did very well,
becoming head chef at the Plaza hotel.
Then he moved out to Cleveland where he opened his own
"Giardino d'Italia", where he became known
as the highly respected recognized dean
of delectable savory Italian cuisine.
Then he opened a plant, but it seems he forgot
when to turn off the oven flame under the pot.
Now will someone please tell me how it can be
that the man we now know as Chef Boy-ar-DEE,
gastronomic maestro, Italiano by birth,
makes the gummiest god-awful pasta on earth.

BUFF ENOUGH

There you were, a year ago, lying in bed,
watching a re-run of Hill Street Blues,
almost eleven, thinking mmm, maybe
ten minutes of Letterman after the news?
And then there they were, with their washboard abs,
each looking super, superbuff, supertrim,
a he and a she, Adonis and Venus,
each on a Power Rod® Bowflex Gym.
Call right now, save over five hundred,
(800) 667-1689,
zero-down financing with low monthly payments,
have your credit card ready, contact us on line.
So you sat at your Mac, Visa in hand,
and ordered it, it came, you used it a lot,
then over the weeks you used it less,
then less and less and less and then not.
And now here you are, outside your garage,
watching yard-hunters poke around and pause
at your snow-blower, end tables, flyrod, canoe,
your microwave, CDs, your box of old saws,
your baby clothes, Legos, video games,
the Wurlitzer juke box you bought on a whim,
and over in the corner, way in the back,
your good-as-new Power Rod® Bowflex Gym.

OCTOGENARIAN BLUES

I could spell from memory phlegm and myrrh,
syzygy, hors d'oeuvres, bouillabaisse,
I was aces at poker, a Scrabble champ,
a past grandmaster at chess.
Mention a name, I knew who it was,
Kate Smith, Lash LaRue, Rudolf Hess,
Soupy Sales, Patti Page, Major Bowes,
Thor Heyerdahl, Eliot Ness.
I did the Saturday Times puzzle with a pen,
it was all so effortless.
But eventually occurred the big eight-O,
and around then, I must confess,
all that lovely acuity began to check out,
and now it's a toil to access
my pin number, parking spot, name of my dog,
each day it's one detail less.
I misplace my glasses, my cell phone, my keys,
sometimes I forget my address.
But the most ironic one is going on now:
I can't find my G.P.S.

Thanks to Rip Rowan.

JENNY

You saw her on a lot on Sunrise Highway,
lit by dangling lightbulbs in the night.
Her price was writ in soap upon her windshield,
but what price love, especially at first sight.
You bargained, earned and borrowed what he wanted,
then drove her home with paeans to the Lord,
the first adult commitment of your young life,
your pretty, necessary Jenny Ford.
Jenny'd had another, maybe more, it didn't matter,
she was instantly responsive to your touch.
Within a day your left foot had discovered
the exact responsive catchpoint of her clutch.
You undid her hood and cleaned and gapped her sparkplugs,
you checked her belts, her fuel pump and her coil,
you replaced one of her lovely headlights,
then you changed her filter and her oil.
On Saturdays you bathed her and you waxed her,
you rubbed til she was candy to the eyes.
At night you went and called on a real girl,
then drove and showed them both off to the guys.

But as time went on, your Jenny got the wearies,
her shock absorbers failed, then her springs.
Her clutch began to slip because her oil leaked
from around her old and worn-out piston rings.
Her water pump quit working, then her fuel pump,
a caliper seized up, her muffler blew,
and that January night she left you stranded,
you sat there in the cold and then you knew.
With a tearful sigh you drove her to the junkyard,
kissed her on the dashboard, said adieu,
then caught a bus ride back to Sunrise Highway,
on the make for Jenny Number Two.

A GOSPEL TRUTH

Inside the close and holy darkness
of Saint Christopher's Church,
twelve-year old Eddie listened raptly
to the Gospel of Saint Luke.
A rich man fires his steward for mismanagement
and the steward laments:
What am I to do?
To dig I am not able,
to beg I am ashamed.
What does he do?
He summons his master's debtors and says
How much do you owe my master?
A hundred jars of oil.
Sit down and write a bond for fifty.
The next one, a hundred bushels of wheat.
Sit down and write eighty.
The master commends the steward and hires him back.
The more I thought about it,
the more I came to understand
that this was very very very good advice.
It still is.

MIDLIFE CRISIS

Yesterday morning I looked in my drawer:
not a square inch for even one sweater more.
Cardigans, jerseys, unworn all
but the one daughter Sally knitted last fall,
that I wear whenever I wear one at all.
For my birthday upcoming, therefore, a request.
If it's not too presumptious, may I suggest
a split case of Burgundy reds and Bordeaux,
a gift card to Borders or Macy's or Lowe's,
tickets to games or plays, anything goes,
but please disallow any notion of clothes.
No bathrobes or neckwear or PJs or hose.
Yet having said that, even any of those
would be better
than yet
another sweater.

UPDATE

The girl from Ipanema
now weighs one eighty-three.
Now each day when she walks to the sea,
she looks at me.

A BUM IN THE BELLY

There's no sleeping pill made,
no trick of the trade,
like rum or the counting of sheep
that can carry a man
like a breast in the hand
and a bum in the belly
to sleep.

FIFTY WORDS THAT WILL SHORTZ CAN'T LIVE WITHOUT

When he's stuck with ELS, there's (thank you) Golfer Ernie.
There's ERLE for Nero's author and HADJ for Muslim journey.
Then there's YMA, UMA, ENO for Sumac, Thurman, Brian,
and ARTE, RHEA, MEG for Johnson, Pearlman, Ryan.
For Once, once, and Racer's edge there's ERST and STP.
For Disney film and Wide shoe size there's TRON and EEE.
Hook's accomplice gives him SMEE and Old-time dagger SNEE,
while Title role for Richard Gere, of course, is DRT.
SNERT is Hagar's comic pooch, altar vow's IDO,
and thank a puzzler's lucky stars for actor Gulager: CLU.
There's Actress Stevens, INGE, and Actress Susan, DEY,
and then of course four times a week, Cosmetics queen ESTEE.
Thanks for Sitcom planet, ORK, and Chinese nurse, AMAH,
for Teenage problem, ACNE, and Island rhythm, SKA,
for Comic Philips, EMO and Melville work, OMOO,
for Shakespeare river, AVON, and for -Acte, ENTR', too.
Poet's inits. are RLS or maybe TSE,
there's Island garland, LEI, and Zeppelin Graf, that's SPEE.
For Battle site there's YSER, or frequently STLO.
There's Paris summer, that's ETE, and Paris water, EAU.
Western Jack is ELAM, yes, and EDAM's Holland cheese,
while Sarge's dog is OTTO and -Gold must be ULEES.
Hawaiian goose is NENE, AJAR's Not open wide,
Norah's dog is ASTA, and NEAP's a Kind of tide,
while ERSE is Old-time Gaelic tongue and OBI's Geisha tie.
Words like Salon substance, GEL, sustain our puzzle guy;
every night at evening prayers as Will looks toward the sky
he thanks Mrs. Morales for naming him ESAI.

JERSEY, NOVEMBER

Rain riverdances on the roof.
It yowled down from Edmonton as snow,
making headlines out of weather reports.
Rudy's on his bed, a furry headless catcurl,
waiting for his Helen's cushy lap.
The ski jacket, promoted to hanger one, waits.
County salt trucks wait to pace-car the roads.
Indoor plants, shivering on the porch,
wait for the door to open.
Soon-to-be Santas wait, accepting seconds on dessert.
The oak has gone downstairs to bed,
blowing off photosynthesis to the pine.
And I am headed upstairs
to await my Helen's splendid bum.

THE AGES OF MAN

1. The Age of Fractions
   Q: How old are you?
   A: I'm five and a half! (5 years, one month)

2. The Age of Anticipation
   Q: How old are you?
   A: I'm going on sixteen! (12)

3. The Age of Accuracy
   Q: How old are you?
   A: I'm twenty-three. (correct)

4. The Age of Evasion
   Q: How old are you?
   A: I'm in my late forties. (52)

5. The Age of Accomplishment
   Q: How old are you?
   A: I just made eighty!

6. The Age of Fractions Redux
   Q: How old are you?
   A: I'm a hundred and one and a half! (101 years, one month)

THIS OLD HOUSE

He has held four dozen children and at least one dozen wives.
He has warmed them and protected all those frail and fecund
    lives.
He was built here where I'm sitting, on a gentle green ascent.
There was no one else for miles then, George the first was
    president.
All those dogs and cats and squirrels, all those quarrels, tears
    and grins,
all those Christmases and Easters, all those prayers and venial
    sins,
all those schoolbooks, bikes and jump ropes,
all those laughs and squeals and shouts,
all those dives beneath the table when the lightning walked
    about.
But.
It appeared his days were numbered in the years of FDR,
with peeling paint and sagging porch, his weedy reedy yard.
He was looking wan and feeble, he was seeming drear and
    old,
his old screens let in the bugs and his old doors let in the cold.
His old fireplace was smoky, his old roof let in the rain,
and he saw an angel peeking through a broken window pane.
Then.
When we paid two hundred thousand for him thirty years
    ago,
oh what toiling, midnight oiling, roiling, little did we know.
We installed new thermal windows, sealed his roof, bought all
    new doors,
we replaced his ancient furnace and redid his baths and
    floors.
Then we modernized his kitchen, fixed his chimney, built a
    shop,
and the yard? Send House and Garden out here for a photo op.

But.
All that sanding, all that weeding, all that sheetrock, all
    those tiles,
all that mowing makes us feel as if we've run a thousand
    miles.
Now his screens keep out the bugs and his new hearth
    defeats the cold,
so while he grows ever younger, she and I, we're growing
    old.
Now he's vigorous and youthful with his comely coats of
    paint,
while my loving wife and I, we're marching on to meet the
    saints.
So.
We will sell him for two million, payback for that sweat
    and strife,
that's one million for a smaller house, one million for our
    life.
To commemorate the beauty, all the artistry and grace,
the exalting transformation that we've brought to this old
    place,
to distinguish us from others, all the rest who came and
    went,
we have printed our initials in a patch of wet cement.

LAST ON LINE

Forty years ago, at 32,
I was asked "Are you gay?"
I smiled naively and said "Sometimes."
He smiled back, inferring a feeler I hadn't meant.
Twenty years ago, at 52,
I was asked "Are you on line?"
I saw a bank, a market checkout.
I smiled and said "Not at the moment."
He smiled back, inferring a drollery I hadn't intended.
Ten years ago, at 62,
I sat down at my first PC,
or, as it served me then, space-age typewriter.
No strikeovers, no Wite-out, no carbons,
but no e-mail either. Too complex.
If you wanted to get in touch, write or phone.
Then, three years ago, at 69,
I got Claudia for Christmas,
instructress extraordinaire.
Linking, scanning, copying, pasting
forwarding, even envelopes, now all routine.
So today, at 72, I can state without ambiguity
"No", and "Yes".

THE RULER OF THE ROAD

The Italian driver slips into his seat,
straps on his belt and turns the key,
screeches out onto the autostrada
and into his morning Grand Prix.
He will flash by them all in his silver Mercedes,
directional screaming, right foot to the floor.
With reluctance the others cede to his will.
He exults; what's testosterone for?
Then off on a side road a little while later,
he's suddenly right behind me.
Expecting defiance he flashes his signal
but then is astonished to see
the car ahead of him pull to the right
with a smile and a friendly wave too.
I didn't come here for Formula One,
I came to admire the view.
He says to himself "Ma come è strano...
gentiluomo, ma non è Italiano."

("How curious that is...
a gentleman, but he's not Italian."

TO ALL YOU WHO REPREHEND IMMIGRANTS

You, Murphy, and you, Pincus, Kazak,
Johnson, Chu, Naguchi, Martínez, Ngo,
Romano, Waslewski, Hassan, Ferguson,
Van Buren, Mboto, Poussin, Anderson,
Romanovich, Schmidt,
all of you pointing the finger of blame,
tell me, which one of those is a Navajo name?

A RECESSION RECOMMENDATION AT THE WINE SHOP

"This is the latest from Oregon.
It is no good with pasta or meat,
or poultry or mushrooms or seafood,
it's not elegant, not elite.
It has no nose, no body, no finish,
no aroma, no bouquet.
It's not arrogant, woody or flinty,
not impudent, bold or risqué.
It's not assertive, not fruity, not spicy,
all in all it is one dreadful wine.
But it does have this going for it:
It's on sale for $4.99."

"I'll take it."

A CHAT WITH THE MAD HATTER

A Tea Partisan in an Uncle Sam hat
had a setup at the mall.
"One moment, sir," said he, beckoning,
"this won't take long at all.
Do you consider yourself a patriot,
a real American, just like me?"
"I do indeed, indeed I do!"
I said most emphatically.
"Well then I'm sure that you'll agree,
our government's out of whack.
With this petition, the message it sends?
We will take our country back.
The constitution of '87
was perfect, word for word.
So bring it back, the way it was!
Sign here and let's be heard!"
"So," said I, "a second chance
to right some serious wrongs?"
"You got it, my man, and this blank space
is where your name belongs!"
"I like it," I said, "but I'd propose
just one small change or two.
This time around, blacks can own whites,
how does that sound to you?
One more thing- in Constitution II
only women are allowed to vote.
That would right two original wrongs,"
said I, and on that note
I winked at his unsmiling face
and said "Think about it! Gotta go!"
He was looking around for Patriot II;
I took that as a no.

CANTERBURY FOLLIES

Anglican churchmen are all in a dither:
One of their bishops is gay.
One man to one woman, not two men,
that's beyond question God's way.
The sanctity of marriage itself is at stake,
can anything be plainer to see?
And Henry the founder, with his six wedded wives,
would doubtlessly all agree.

HAIKU

MAÑANA ES OTRO DÍA

Tomorrow morning,
if you wake, then you will have
one more chance at it.

MARRIED ONE MONTH

mums on the table,
new curtains on the windows,
bras on the doorknobs

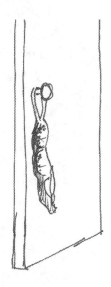

TEENS ENTER A RESTAURANT

Which table, she asks
Why don't you choose, he replies:
young, yet so, so wise

MARY, TO THE LITTLE DRUMMER BOY

He just fell asleep,
so, dear boy, you and your drum,
will you please beat it.

A SIGN OF HYPOCRISY

on the front door of
the Jehovah's Witnesses:
NO SOLICITING

THE SEVENTH DECADE

for Tom Fricke

All of the names in
my little black book end with
the letters M.D.

PRIVATE MOMENTS

Beware the man who,
alone with a tea cozy,
does not try it on.

NONEGENARIAN ENTERS A RESTAURANT

Waiter, if you please,
I'd like a table near the
defibrillator.

THUS IT HAS EVER BEEN

a primary source
of temporal elation:
that first morning pee

APRÈS PEE

barefooting it back,
feeling chilly, embracing
my wife's warm round bum

LUCK

Like a Russian car,
the only time that it works
is when you push it.

FIFTH GRADE CHRISTMAS PAGEANT

The Virgin's robe is
dullish grey but her toenails
are painted bright red.

AT FIFTY

Some day we'll look back,
back at these years of our lives,
and draw a big blank.

IF I HAD GONE INTO THE PRIESTHOOD

Today I might be
Edward Cardinal Caffrey...
mm... maybe... mm... nah.

DAVID ORECK

He's a nice guy but
all he ever talks about
is vacuum cleaners.

ON THE THIRTEENTH DAY OF CHRISTMAS

The whole caboodle
went up for sale on eBay,
every leaping lord.

CONUNDRUM

I've lost my glasses
and I won't know where to look
until I find them.

HELEN AND MICKEY

Helen smiled when she
found her bra in our puppy's bed,
a sure sign of love.

PENNIES

Just one would buy you a Tootsie Roll
from the penny candy tray.
Three of them bought you a first-class stamp,
that's forty-four today.
One for a picture postcard,
"Having fun, wish you were here."
That's cheaper than an e-mail,
and a classier souvenir.
We inserted them into our loafers
(rich kids inserted dimes).
It was five for the Daily News
and ten for the New York Times.
One would buy you a gumball
or into a poker game,
five for a Nathan's hot dog
of Coney Island fame.
One once would buy you a share of stock,
though distinctly lower grade.
A bunch would buy you an hour of fun
at the downtown penny arcade.
But think-- is there anything whatsoever
you can buy for a penny today?
When you drop one you say Never Mind,
and you let it roll away.
But I was the kid buying Tootsie Rolls,
can't even remember how many,
so drop one and watch me, I will
bend over and pick up that penny.

EX-SUPERMODEL FINDS NEW WORK

Here in my sixties, which my husband calls
the top of the seventh inning,
after a long life in front of a lens,
I've begun my second beginning.
I once posed for Gucci, Van Cleef and Arpels,
for Lanvin and Comme Des Garçons,
for Isaac Mizrahi and Yves Saint Laurent,
Versace and Louis Vuitton.
But my young immortality lost to reality,
I slipped from designers to stores.
Now Nieman and Bloomie's and Macy's and Saks,
no more Laurens or Christian Diors.
Then in my forties I slipped even further
(there's no way to contradict years)
to the Wilmington Boat Show and Sleep Number Beds,
Lens Crafters, Playtex and Sears.
Then through my fifties my agent forgot
what a star I once was in the biz.
He somehow or other misplaced my phone number
and in the end I misplaced his.
But shout halleluja, I've a whole new career,
as far as can be from Lancôme,
I'm paying my half of the rent by pole dancing
at the Feathered Nest Old People's Home.

BAD LANGUAGE

You can say cazzo about anywhere,
in Poland, Japan or Dubai.
Shout it out loud in Rwanda,
nobody bats an eye.
But whisper it softly in Roma,
matronly tongues will click,
because cazzo in Roma is weenie,
pecker, dink, johnson, dick.
Five letters freighted with evil,
conveying disparagement of
that upstanding society member,
the purple-helmeted warrior of love.
Each of the George Carlin no-nos,
words that Jim Lehrer can't say,
is a source of gratification
in its own particular way:
a pleasureful dump in the morning,
the organs of marital bliss.
You can say rape and torture on TV,
but under no circumstance piss.
Well, shit. I have a proposal
after thinking it over a lot.
Let's decriminalize all of those no-nos,
beginning with... mm, let's see... twat.
But inFLUence, eviDENTly, I could care less,
between you and I, sort of, you know,
that's what is truly bad language,
that is what has to go.

THE SEVEN DEADLY SINS

Years ago some lust, but gluttony,
avarice, wrath, pride and envy,
surprisingly little for a man not of the cloth.
But I am looking forward to a dotage
of glorious well-earned sloth.

HUMMERDINK

It is hard scientific fact,
as the atmosphere of Venus is,
that the owners of very large cars
have among the world's smallest penises.

THIS JUST IN FROM LONDON

British Health Services have announced that
Brits are growing uncommonly fat.
My only question is just this: Who'd
have thought they could do it on English food?

FEBRUARY BLUES

Like a dungeoned wretch,
haggard and gaunt,
proffering a mendicant's spoon,
I scan the sports pages,
buoyed by the hope
that baseball will start again soon.

DAIRY LAW THWARTS ROMANCE

Scene one: I'm eleven, sitting at the kitchen table,
kneading a pound of margarine.
Parkay, I think, or was it Kraft? Blue Bonnet?
Butter had gone to war and the dairy states,
fearful of permanent conversions,
had legislated colorless margarine. White like lard,
until you pinched the red capsule in the plastic sac
and kneaded the color in, slowly, ever yellower and warmer.
It was a chore I was fond of, though I didn't know why.

Scene two: I'm sixteen, in the back seat of her parents' Buick.
She kindly unhooks her strapless bra
and there are two chubby titties, the first I've ever seen,
soft and white, ready for fondling.
But as I do, a kitchen memory creeps in...
two pounds of warm Parkay.
I break the kiss, laughing.
She breaks away crying, rehooks and runs.

In a fairy tale conclusion, I never again would have dated,
fearful of a replay.
Not true, I've had a lovely life,
but I've never once gone to Wisconsin.

BASEBALL 2020, A PROPHESY

The first pitch of the ballgame is low and away, ball one.
The first name in muffler care is Aamco, double A, MCO.
Martín is a sinker-slider pitcher with an ERA
of six, because his so-called fastball is just so-so.
Next pitch, a line drive to center, and speaking of drive,
have you driven a Ford lately? Well why not do it today?
The pitch to Melvin misses, but don't you miss
the summertime bargains at your Tri-State Chevrolet.
Here's the manager now, it looks like Martín is done,
after a hit-filled, walk-filled three-inning stint.
He's calling for a lefty, number forty, Pedro Moreno.
This call to the bullpen is brought to you by Sprint.
Moreno's first pitch, a drive to the left field wall...
It's a...
    Wendy's Wallop/Big Mac Smack/Burger King Dinger/
    Bud Blast/Schlitz Schmash/Pabst Poke/
    Miller Miler/Dockers' Rocket/Samsonite 4-Bagger (get it?)
home run ball!
Be sure to tune in tomorrow night at seven,
when your friendly Long Island Kia dealers present
the Yankees, and don't forget, a fifteen-minute
call to Geico can save you fifteen percent!

SOUP FOR SALE

Campbell's Soup, 1930, 12¢ a can:
pepper pot, consommé, ox-tail and
chicken, asparagus, bean, beef and pea,
julienne, mulligatawny, celery,
bouillon, printanier (a dark horse),
mutton, mock turtle and tomato, of course.

BEAUTY OVER DUTY

On the cesspool's rim, portulaca;
opulent, vivid, dramatic,
jellybeanishly polychromatic,
the efflorescence of caca.

I

I am super hyper important to 1 person.
I am super important to 2 other persons.
I am very very important to 12 other persons.
I am very important to 34 other persons.
I am important to 61 other persons.
I am utterly unimportant to 6,830,047,141 other persons.
I like the numbers.

WINTER THROUGH THE AGES

Ages 5-10
    Freezing in bed at night
    under every last blanket plus a throw rug,
    a cat under the covers, grateful for each other,
    expanding an inch at a time,
    body-warming the arctic sheets.
    Shoveling snow with a coal shovel,
    too heavy for a skinny kid,
    runny nose, flu, we called it the grippe,
    helping my mother haul out the ashes,
    the cans were steel, not plastic.
    My father? On a stool at the Village Tavern.
    Plodding to school in galoshes that leaked,
    socks soaking wet and cold,
    a coat with a hood, not quite thick enough,
    walking backward into the wind.
    But.
    Snowmen, snowballs, sleds, sliding on the ice,
    and Christmas.

Ages 10-15
    Delivering Newsdays in snowfalls so thick
    I could barely see the porches,
    walking my bike through drifts,
    frozen laundry on the line,
    and still the freezing bed, warm cat.
    But.
    Sledding on the frozen creeks,
    snowball battles from 6-foot snowforts,
    and Christmas.

Ages 20-60
Icy windshields, large oil bills,
frozen pipes, slippery roads,
shoveling, shoveling, shoveling,
car won't start, kids with colds,
streets not plowed, friends moving to Florida.
But.
Sleighrides with family, skiing in New Hampshire,
roaring fireplaces, snuggling with Helen,
greeting card winter vistas, skating on the pond,
romping in the snow with a short-legged dog,
and Christmas.

Ages 70-?
Eyeglasses fog up, lower back hurts,
walking the dog in a blizzard, eyelashes caked with snow,
aluminum snowshovel heavier each year,
too dark too soon, too much night driving,
still more frozen pipes and larger oil bills,
more friends gone to Florida,
grippe now flu, cold wind down your neck,
hazardous roads, black ice and slush,
powerouts, so no cooking or flushing,
no heat, so back to the bed with the arctic sheets.
But.
Now there's a warm-bodied wife instead of a cat,
and Christmas.

PROGRESS IN BIOLOGY

In 1949 I got a C.
Thirty years later,
my daughter got a Ph.D.

WHY IS IT THAT

Patrick Dempsey incarnates sex
with a beard of several days,
while I, unshaven just as long,
resemble Gabby Hayes?

WINDBREAKERS

Lady Gaga farts with gusto,
as do Oprah and Mo'Nique,
while Dr. Dre and Yo-Yo Ma
much prefer the one-cheek sneak.

Peons and potentates fart,
dormitory roomates fart,
puppies and primates fart,
Bill and Melinda Gates fart.

Le Pétomane, a stage sensation,
wowed the crowds in old Paree,
emitting a range of broken winds
from deep bassoon to chickadee.

Napoleon Bonaparte farted,
René Descartes farted,
Richard the Lionheart farted,
Amadeus Mozart farted.

A fart in a bar elicits a laugh:
Don't look at me! Not Me! That was you!
That's why a fart is redolent,
so deaf people can enjoy it too.

NUMBER 11

Lean and silent, ambling softly, unobserved,
idling in neutral, not a calorie misspent,
sensing, anticipating... Now.
At full speed in two steps,
he burgles a boy who never saw him coming.
Dancing the ball past two more,
he feeds it to the foot of a friend,
then races for the feedback.
A whistle. Ball out of bounds.
Eleven holds it high,
then springs, flips, catapults it,
a 35-yard arc onto the flurry in the box.
A friendly forehead flicks it in.
A minute later, where'd he go?
Ah, there, in nimble amble,
just beyond the radar.

for Warren Kimber IV
by Edward Caffrey II,
November, 2005

AMERICAN BANKING

Don't have a credit rating, can't get a loan.
They punch me up, screen says no, applicant unknown.
The elemental problem is, I've never had a loan.
Never had to borrow, always paid it on my own.
Every bank will say no if you've never had a loan,
they look at you aghast, as they did with Al Capone.
What, you're American and never had a loan?
Do you think that is something our system can condone?
Oh well.
If there ever comes a day when I really need a loan,
I'll just sit down and call Paulie Walnuts on the phone.

GAY MEN, COME ON UP!

In 1202, Jesus appeared to Jean-Paul in Marseille.
"Do not," said He, "reveal how I have judged Judas,
lest my mercy be abused."
He judged him by welcoming him at the gate,
saying "Good job well done."
Judas had been programmed,
as have gay men.
Gay is not le mot juste
to describe the boy
who lusts for the quarterback
while other boys leer at the cheerleaders.
It's not gay but it is there.
And Who, do you suppose, put it there?
Note that's Who with a capital W.

QUICK QUAKER OATS

Depending on the distance from payday,
there might be Wheaties for breakfast,
or Chex, the subcompact Shredded Wheat,
or Force, each box bearing a presidential coin, 32 in '43,
or Kix. I told someone I got mine on Route 66;
she said she got hers at A&P.
And save that box. There were Mustangs, Thunderbolts,
Avengers, three pieces to snip, attach, glide.
And send in the top, a trinket for a 3-cent stamp.
But. As the month ran out, so did the money,
and so did the Wheaties.
One of those mornings, a pause on the stairs...
What was on the stove-- was it welcome Wheatena
or dreaded oatmeal? A sniff and you knew... no aroma...
oatmeal. I can taste it now, shredded paper in warm milk
that no amount of sugar could redeem.
It's been said that, as with margarine and liver,
anyone who once had to eat it never never will again.
So please, Wilford Brimley,
you and your apple-cheeked friend in the flat hat,
don't bother me, I'm eating my Wheaties.

TO TIMOTHY CARDINAL DOLAN, SAINT PATRICK'S CATHEDRAL

About the Saint...
He was born of Roman parents
in the colony of Britain
in the year 387,
or so his history's written.
He was snatched by Irish pirates,
a boy of just sixteen,
and sold to tend his master's flocks
in the hills near Ballygreen.
But he dropped his crook and beat it,
back to Britain, on to Gaul,
to return one day to Erin
as the holiest of all.
He's the symbol of the Emerald Isle,
from Derry down to Cork.
The Irish built a church for him
in then-uptown New York.
It bears his name, Tim Dolan,
and it's now your Holy See.
But adjustments now are needed
to set straight his history.
Rearrange the marching groups
in the Patty's Day Parade.

Ask the hordes of Irish
to accept a mild downgrade.
One step to the rear,
you lads from County Clare,
and move back all those banners
from Roscommon and Kildare.
one step back, Tyrone Brigade,
and you, Kenmare Batallion.
To the front, you Sons of Italy,
Saint Patrick was Italian.

WHY ENGLISH IS THE HARDEST LANGUAGE TO LEARN

It started out as German, which was sat upon by French,
a French approximated by assimilated Danes
who came from up the coast from where the Saxon Germans
     came;
the Danish French and Saxon German never quite
     homogenized.
Homogenize, approximate, assimilate retain
their Latinate hauteur, remaining grandly out of reach
of man and house and cat and mouse and gross.
And so when English jumped ship here it was already plump
with synonyms, redundancies or pleonasms, take your pick.
There's fast and rapid, late and tardy, small and petty, far
     and distant,
and and also too, as well.
Irish swelled it even further, Yiddish, Spanish, Finnish too,
and African, Italian and Chinese:
Think donnybrook and hooligan, mazeltov and schmuck,
rodeo, taco, sauna, goober, ciao, and wok.
Then there's yo bro from the ghetto and howdy pard from
     Dodge,
and brand name words like Kleenex, Coke, Scotch Tape and
     Vaseline.
They make our dictionary now the heaviest of any printed
in the western world – a trial for learners but a trove for poets.
Just imagine: 24 words for auto in the book of synonyms,
63 for fool, and for buttocks 38 – that's 28 plus 10 I added,
not found in the thesaurus, a word, as often noted,
which has no synonym.

DISILLUSION I

"The weed of crime bears bitter fruit;"
the Shadow said, "crime does not pay."
The Shadow and Green Hornet saw to that,
the FBI in Peace and War, Dick Tracy, Captain Marvel,
Batman and his boy and Superman,
and Gangbusters, they busted gangs, dragged felons off in
    cuffs
to cleanse this land of evil every afternoon and night,
880 on the dial, page fifty in the News.
But then I started reading other pages, one and two and
    three,
chronicles of crime and evil that somehow had eluded
all my heroes, and I knew. It was all a hoax
to make me eat their cereal and send away for rings.
My second disillusion after Santa Claus, four years before.
Joe Friday never blew a case,
or Karl Malden on his San Francisco beat.
It wasn't until Hill Street Blues
that the law began to lose one here and there.
If only I had known that then,
I could have reconciled page fifty with page one.

DISILLUSION II

It was dicey for a while there,
but Cinderella finally nailed her prince and lived,
oh reassuring words for a trillion little girls,
happily ever after.
It was the exit line for every tale,
a safe conduct pass to dreamland.
Snow White, Rapunzel, Sleeping Beauty,
all survived the menaces, the stepmaternal treacheries,
to join Prince Charming at the altar,
splendid in Venetian lace.
Then happily ever after, end of story, pleasant dreams.
Another hoax. A well-intentioned hoax,
like Santa and the Shadow,
but cruel, because too soon thereafter,
the prince broke wind at breakfast
and tears came rolling down.
"It's not supposed to be this way," she wept into her toast.
Maybe if he'd cut one as he bent to fit her shoe,
they'd have gone to dreamland wiser,
all those trillion little girls,
and centuries of disillusion tears
would have had no cause to fall.

DISILLUSION III

We owned each other then.
In 40s-50s high school, possession was a must.
Or so they said.
Jo Stafford staked her claim in no uncertain terms:
"Just remember, darling, all the while, you belong to me."
Buddy Clark located ownership: "You belong to my heart."
Don Cornell signed a two-word surrender: "I'm yours."
Ezio Pinza sang the stalkers' song:
"Once you have found her, never let her go."
That's barring a restraining order,
but restraint is what they seldom sang about:
"Forever and ever our love will be true."
Perry Como upped the ante: "Till the end of time".
Our songs were full of promises beyond all feasibility:
"If they made me a king I'd still be a slave to you."
"Everything I have is yours."
But we believed them, and so expected. Hoax number
        three.
But they were on the radio, sung by stars,
sponsored, à propos of hoaxes, by Lucky Strike.
Wasn't that a little bit like being in the paper?
"When you wish upon a star, your dreams come true."
False and misleading, a misdemeanor, but we believed,
and married the girl from English class.
"They tried to tell us we're too young."
They were the they we should have listened to.

WORDS BEFORE NAMES

Big John, Mama Cass, Doctor Phil, Prince Hal,
Uncle Sam, Sir Paul, Aunt Jemima, Weird Al.

Think of all the words that might precede your name.
Here are some of mine; let's see if they're the same.

WERE AND ARE
Uncle Ed, Cousin Ed, Mister Ed (of course, of course)

MIGHT HAVE BEEN
Father Ed (problem: girls), Brother Ed (same),
Officer Ed, Captain Ed, Farmer Ed, Doctor Ed

UNLIKELY BUT POSSIBLE
Judge Ed, Monsignor Ed (see Father), Mayor Ed

IMPOSSBLE
Sir Ed, Don Ed, Big Ed, Pastor Ed, Lord Ed,
Prince Ed, Rabbi Ed

UTTERLY INCONCEIVABLE
Chef Ed

Chef Mario, Chef Pierre, Chef Franz, Chef Julia,
Chef Emeril? Fine, who would doubt it?
Chef Lidia, Chef Tell, even Chef Boyardee,
but Chef Ed? Fuggedaboutit.

ARMAGEDDON

Some say Armageddon's coming soon,
possibly next month.
It's all in the Bible, they claim,
excruciatingly clear.
But Catholics don't read the Bible,
we read the Church Bulletin.
So.
No questions about Armageddon, please,
But Sunday's bake sale? Fire away.

TWENTY

to granddaughter Casey Sullivan Kimber on her twentieth

They say that twenty-one
is the one that changes everything, but no.
Twenty changes just as much, a year before.
Your bed is home but your mind is moving out,
already underway to something else, somewhere else.
Distant forms are taking shape,
like an image filling in
while the blue computer bar snakes across the bottom of
     the screen,
and familiar faces fade, to be seen again at sixty,
over nametags at reunions, at resorts.
But the constants that your mind is full of
will help you sort the forms out as they form,
triage the gentle from the venal,
judge the beneficial from the vain.
Constants in the making twenty years--
loving laughing, loving puppies, loving music,
loving family, loving where you're going.
They'll hold you high and catch you when you fall,
like Daddy waiting as you jumped off from the table,
about, oh, eighteen years ago.

A THOUGHT

In 1200, when they passed out surnames,
three categories were big.
    1. profession: John Carter, John Carpenter, John Taylor
    2. place of abode: John Hill, John Fields, John Rivers
    3. parent: John Johnson, John Jackson, John Peterson.

Imagine if they passed them out today.
    1. John Programmer, John Telemarketer, John Astronaut
    2. John Condo, John Crackhouse, John Fematrailer
    3. John Elvisson, John Mittson, John LeBronson

TRAFFIC REPORT

Scene: roadside, Wantagh, New York, 1959

Dramatis personae: Carolee Caffrey, 2, darling firstborn daughter of Edward Caffrey, 26.

They are watching traffic pass by.

EC: Car.

CC: Ca.

EC: Truck.

CC: Tuk.

EC: Bus.

CC: Bus.

Now a trailer hauling nine new cars passes.

CC: Bus for ca.

EC: Wow... WOW!

DOCTOR CAWEE

(tune similar to She'll Be Comin' Round the Mountain)

(Note: When she was a year old, Carolee supposed that
all other children plus all animals were also named
Cawee Caffwee.)

Cawee Caffwee who lives on Booka Wane
lends boys and girls and pussycats her name.
She can count from one to three
sitting on her Daddy's knee,
and teaches bio at UCLA.

Doctor CL of UCLA
started kindergarten yesterday.
Did a prize-winning paper
on animal behavior,
and finger-painted fishies in the bay.

My brilliant baby Doctor Carolee,
I see you now at 6 and 12 and 3.
You are and were and will be
nobility and beauty,
and once-a-life first baby love to me.

WAKEUP CALL

Scene: master bedroom, Saturday, 6:30 a.m.

Dramatis personae: Sally Caffrey, 2.
Her day cannot begin without her darling Daddy,
Edward Caffrey, 31.

SC: Dad.

EC: Mm.

SC: Dad. Haf deddup.

EC: Okay, soon.

four minutes later

SC: Dad.

EC: Mm.

SC: Haf deddup.

EC: Mm.

two minutes later

SC: Dad.

EC: Mm.

SC: HAF DEDDUP!

I doddup.

SALLY

a song to a daughter on her wedding day,
to the tune of "Easy Winners" by Scott Joplin,
as played by Max Morath

The angel who presided at her birth
said Little baby born of joy and mirth,
bring love to every creature that you meet on earth.
Sally,
when often you come to mind,
images swim in review.
Baby,
running to greet me home,
scratched knees and missing one shoe.
Midnight,
I peek in to watch you sleep,
bottom arched up in a U,
I lay covers of kisses
soft on your baby cheek,
then bow down and thank Him for you.
Uncles
and cousins and waitresses,
grandmas and movie stars too,
still feel the glow on their inner lives
long after Sally passed through.
Babies
        and nasty old men,
even kittens and puppies knew
they were mortally stricken, no antidote,
it was love at first being with you.

I see their faces now
and I remember how
helpless they felt
and how I laughed to myself
Knowing that like me they never had a chance
with the angel of seduction in plastic pants.
Pictures
that look down from on the wall
tell of an angel who grew.
Now look- you're all grown and beautiful,
married and starting off new.
Still though,
when sometimes my fortunes fail
and Mondays turn gloomy blue,
I look up at your face
smiling back down at me
and think of that missing white shoe.
I look up at that face
that always brought joy to me,
and thank Him one more time for you.

90?

Ancestor Eoghan O'Sullivan,
large and fiery of beard and eye,
eluded the Romans, packed his clan on barques,
sailed from Brest to the Kenmare River,
where the indigenes took him for a god;
he accepted their tribute.
He lived, says legend, to a fabled age.
We'll say 90.
Great granduncle Michael O'Leary
passed up potatoes and raised cows.
He survived the blight and lived to 92.
Great grandfather James Sullivan
emigrated to Holyoke, a mill town,
where he opened a grocery.
While the mill workers were choking on lint,
he was packing up potatoes and poteen.
He got to 93.
And that's the men.
The women outlived them all.
So. The genes are there.
Possibly the wits.

FRUSTRATION DEFINED: ASKING AN IRISH FARMER FOR DIRECTIONS

Should you err in the back roads of Sligo,
it would be a momentous mistake
to pull to the side and inquire
of the feller there wielding the rake.
He won't tell you he's really not certain
how to get to the town of Rathcoole.
You see, that would make him look foolish,
and yourself too, for asking a fool.
So he'll say Straightaway, you can't miss it,
it can't be but nine or ten miles.
Then he'll give you a touch to his hatbrim
and you'll drive away thankful, all smiles.
Or you might want the main road to Dingle,
it said left at the last intersection.
He'll say Yessir, the right road it is, sir,
but it isn't the right direction.
One time I said Beg your pardon,
Is this the way to Donegal?
He said Well now meself, sir,
sure, I wouldn't start from here at all.

PUPPY LOVE

Wrinkles, sparse hair, liver spots
are things he doesn't see,
and if Brad and Angelina called him,
still he'd run to me.

A TRUISM

A dog's being rubbed on his belly,
four paws in the air, canine bliss.
The rubber will always intone a refrain,
three times over, something like this:
"Is oo my sweet wittoo puppy?" (once)
"Is oo my sweet wittoo puppy?" (twice)
But twice is never enough. Here it comes:
"Is oo my sweet wittoo puppy?" (thrice)
Never fails.

CRUSHES

in chronological order,
a love poem

Mommy
Mrs. Holler, second grade teacher
Miss Lanigan, sixth grade teacher
Joan Fontaine
Donna Reed
Kim Novak
Helen
Helen
Helen
category retired

RIGHT OR WRONG?

You can't see the Great Wall of China from the moon.
Mount Everest is not the tallest peak.
The Chinese did not invent the rickshaw.
America was named for Richard Ameryk.
Abner Doubleday never saw Cooperstown.
Marco Polo never left Venice, and,
the largest living thing of all is a mushroom.
No ostrich buries his head in the sand.
Raindrops are spheroid, not tear-shaped.
Do St. Bernards carry brandy? No way.
The best conducting metal is silver.
The home of the most tigers? The U.S. of A.
Caesar was not born by Caesarean section.
Nero never fiddled, just think why:
The fiddle was invented 15 centuries later.
Your nails and hair don't grow when you die.
Atlas carried the heavens, not the earth.
The feminists never burned a bra.
Violin strings were never of catgut.
George's teeth wood? Another faux pas.
The Canary Islands were named for dogs.
Pérignon invented champagne? A tall tale.
The Emperor's thumbs-UP meant the gladiator died.
Jonah couldn't possibly have been swallowed by a whale.
How'd you do?
If you said they're all right
then you got them all right.
Good for you.

A GROUCH IN THE MAKING

I know more about
Chiquita Banana than Hannah Montana,
Ben-Gay than Dr. Dre,
Captain Cook than Facebook,
hot rods than iPods,
banana splits than mosh pits,
Ben Grauer than Matt Lauer,
Nathan's Franks than Tyra Banks,
J. Paul Getty than Ugly Betty,
Sam I Am than Pearl Jam,
Phineas Fogg than Snoop Dogg,
Jiffy Lube than You Tube,
Doris Day than eBay,
Tom Carvel than AOL,
Al Capone than iPhone,
Frank Nitti than P. Diddy,
Bronx cheers than Britney Spears,
BVDs than DVDs,
Cracker Jacks than Betamax,
bumper cars than VCRs,
Roddy McDowall than Simon Cowell,
Al Capp than Gangsta rap,
ancient Greeks than Wikileaks,
Rag Mop than hip hop or Iggy Pop,
Tiny Tim than Lil Kim,
Buffalo Bill than Doctor Phil,
and that's the way I like it.
Hmpf.

THERE MUST BE SOMETHING...

High top shoes, nutcracker, kids' potty chair,
Mouseketeer ears, Union Suit underwear,
Lincoln Logs, roller skates, skeleton key,
ice cream scoop, BB gun, where can it be?
A Flexible Flyer or cowpuncher chaps,
Tootsie Toys, where, in the attic perhaps?
A Lionel train car, a souvenir spoon,
a cardboard hearth or a brass spittoon,
a Slinky, corn plaster, a stuffed Yogi Bear,
someplace in this old house I know that there
is something I bought forty-five years ago
that is now worth a wad on the Antiques Road Show.

ONE FOR THREE

Wanted to pich for the Yankees.
Couldn't.
Accurate but slow.
Hmm, accurate but slow:
high-arc softball.
Won 538 games.

Wanted to write movie scripts.
Couldn't.
Ideations clever but way too short.
Hmm, clever but short:
television commercials.
Won 14 Clios.

Wanted a beautiful, smart, funny,
tender-hearted woman.
Her name is Helen Caffrey.

THESE ARE QUITE A FEW OF MY FAVORITE THINGS

Rubbing my cute little puppy dog's belly
to the soaring strains of Andrea Bocelli,
Roger Angell, Red Smith, Click and Clack, NPR,
a green '40 Ford, my teenage first car,
my Lionel trains, my wee Tootsietoys,
Hershey Bars, Mounds, and best, Almond Joys,
my ultrasplendiferous Schwinn maroon bike,
throwing a baffling high-arching strike,
the Joe Torre Yankees, the Tom Seaver Mets,
the Bill Parcells Giants, the Joe Namath Jets,
Marlon in Streetcar, Alan in Shane,
Paul in The Hustler, Burt in The Train,
watching the Yanks win at Fenway Park,
watching my 2-year old dance to Dick Clark,
stickball played with a beatup Spaldeen,
High Noon, Two Women, The African Queen,
my first hearing Carmen, my first raise in pay,
Wait, Wait, Don't Tell Me and Garrison K,
Hank the Cinq, Hamlet, Lear and Othello,
James Durante and Louis Costello,
Blondie, Prince Valiant, the Shadow, Dick Tracy,
Daniel Day-Lewis and William H. Macy,
the Bionic Woman, the Man of Steel,
the all-time best admen, the Brothers Piel,

softball and bocce, hoseshoes and darts,
Scrabble and Jeopardy!, poker and hearts,
Lacrima Cristi or Côtes du Rhône wine,
Brooks and Dionne, Maureen Dowd and Joe Klein,
ER and Hill Street, NYPD Blue,
taking my girls to the Central Park Zoo,
Crosby, of course, Sinatra I guess,
Elvis, forget it, Mel Tormé yes,
Little Phil, Yogi, The Mick and Joe D.,
Earl the Pearl, Willis, Clyde, Dave deB.,
a Mozart concierto, a Scott Joplin rag,
a John Steinbeck novel, a Jay Leno gag,
all those laughs, Jackie G., Milton B.,
Victor B., Richard P., Billy C., Lily T.,
the Patty's Day show we put on every year,
after a hot game, an antarctic beer,
the County of Kerry, Matera, Marseille,
the first man I cried for, my fine JFK,
my first house, my first dog, my first ring, my first date,
the first love of my life, my sweet Mommy Kate,
watching my Kimmie play soccer, hearing my Casey sing
watching my Raven excel at just about everything,
my beautiful girls, the lights of my life,
and my gorgeous and brilliant and sweet-hearted wife.

THE LAST GRAD, CLASS OF '31

There were 212 in the class photo then,
each a fresh-faced last-day twelfth grader.
We reuned at a lodge in the Pocono hills
one day 25 years later.
We'd put on a little around the middle
and lost considerable off the top,
but of the 212, almost all were still there
to convene for the photo op.
For 50, about half showed up for the pic,
a hundred or so, maybe more.
And, oh sobering sight, the lodge had installed
a defibrillator there by the door.
60 and 70 came and went
with sharp drops in alum celebrators.
Now, at our 80th reunion the photo
is down to me and two waiters.

IN PURSUIT OF THE ELUSIVE ENIGMATIC MEANING OF LIFE

Sometimes I feel like the Sheriff
in "Smokey and the Bandit",
chasing that semi full of Coors
from Colorado to Texas,
across state lines,
often in the opposing lane,
down a hillside, bang, lost a hubcap,
up an arroyo, whoop, there goes the hood,
under a culvert, duck, crunch, one less roof.
He makes it to Texas, and I to 75,
diminished but persistent...
now which way did that sumbitch go?

ACCESSIBLE VERSATILITY
a sonnet of sorts

The verse before this one, the one you've just read,
is mildly amusing and certainly terse,
but it has no meter and doesn't rhyme,
so it can't be a poem, only a verse.
There are poetry teachers who will insist
that rhyme's not required all of the time,
citing Whitman and Auden and Pound, but I'm
an English major and I say that rhyme
is essential to poetry, so some of my words
are called verses, not poems, since that leaves me free
to follow the forms or form my own;
contrived or classic, it's all up to me.
Meter and rhyme? Maybe so, maybe not.
Call it a verse, you get away with a lot.

AN ENGLISH MAJOR'S GUIDE TO FALLING ASLEEP

Number one, make a list, e.g. "rhymes with oon".

A afternoon
B buffoon, bassoon... Brigadoon!
C cartoon? Cancún!
D doubloon... not bad
E tough one... E... ex-something... excommune!
F festoon
G goon? too easy... gossoon
H harvest moon? honeymoon
I I... in, im something? importune
J June? no... jejune
K K... that place in China... Kowloon!
L mmm... lagoon, lacune, lampoon
M gotta be monsoon... or macaroon
N noon, too easy... Neptune
O only one, octoroon
P poltroon, pantaloon... picayune
Q only one, quadroon
R Rangoon
S spoon, Saskatoon, spittoon... starting to slip away...
T T, as in tired... T... typhoon
U unsomething... untune? good enough
V very soon... very soon...
W weary... OK, one last one... Walloon
X forget it
Y Y, that's what I say, why?
Z zzzzz

BEHIND THE WATCHTOWER

Let me tell you the story of Charles Taze Russell,
a grifter the cops called Charlie Hustle.
In the opening years of the century past,
he preached that our world was fading fast.
He said Armageddon was close at hand,
so come and join his sanctified band.
The rest of the world was sinful, depraved;
Jehovah's Witnesses alone would be saved.
You won't need your belongings after the crash,
so sell them all now and give Charlie the cash.
As each prophesied Doomsday arrived and passed,
all Charlie did was revise his forecast:
Five months away is the new Day of Woe,
in the meantime, keep forking over the dough.
If that made any sense, however bizarrely,
there was one other clause in the Gospel of Charlie
that defied credibility: Article Seven.
Only 144 thou go to heaven.
It's there, I saw it, I read it, it's true.
So here is the question that I have for you:
If somehow, some way you believed in this hoax,
would you be out there soliciting folks?
Not me, I'd say People, let's keep this to us-
there are only 8 seats left on the bus!
Pull down the shades, let's sit tight and wait.
Oh, what was that new Apocalypse date?

THE BANNS

When Sean and Norah vowed to wed,
they made it known to all concerned,
families and friends of course,
and dutifully, to Father Burns.
He passed the word to Bishop Flynn,
who published notice of their plans
for three weeks prior to the date,
an ancient rite known as the banns.
If anyone had reason why
they should not be allowed to wed,
let him come forward at this time
and say the words that need be said:
"He has a mistress in Kenmare,
and, so I hear, a baby son."
"She had a fling with Brendan Kelly,
who knows what they might have done?"
It's mostly jilted lovers' malice;
in any case it's washed away
by a full and true confession
prior to the wedding day.
Spread the word, see what turns up,
that was our ancestors' way,
but cell phones and the internet
have nearly banished banns today.
With Google, Facebook, MySpace, Twitter,
everybody in the room
knows as much and maybe more
about the bride than does the groom.
And, Helen adds, a wifely aside,
about the groom as does the bride.

THE DEATHBED CONFESSION OF THE GRANDSON OF GOD

Sun Myung Moon, 90, Tells All

It was at a ceremony in Washington, I remember it well,
in March of the year two thousand and four,
that I, the Reverend Sun Myung Moon,
on the U.S. Senate Office Building floor,
stood, strode forth and held forth at the mike,
severely balding and somewhat obese,
and awarded myself, to some scattered applause,
the yes, self-crafted "Crown of Peace".
> I said "I was sent to Earth to save the world's
> six billion people. Emperors, kings and presidents
> have declared to all Heaven and Earth that
> Reverend Sun Myung Moon is none other than
> humanity's Savior, Messiah, Returning Lord
> and True Parent."

I was raised in a Korean Confucian family,
which, when I was ten, switched to Christianity.
One day I climbed a hill just to see what I could see.
What I saw was Jesus, and here's what He said to me:
> "I appear to you today, my God-appointed son,
> to tell you that my holy work was never wholly done.
> Go forth now, Sun my son, from this bleak Korean hill,
> and bring peace to all the Earth, that is My Almighty Will."

Now I lie here on this bed as they empty out my pan,
and I'm wracked with guilt, wretched with doubt.
I have led my minions, my millions of Moonies
my true-hearted faithful, devoted, devout,
away from the path of salvation and truth,

away from Christianity.
Away from You, down the path of perdition,
to worship the falsest of false Gods, me.

I virtually never mentioned Your name.
I took your place, I was All.
In all of my churches all over the world
my image, not Yours, hung on the wall.
I was fat, I was rich, I was greedy, I was lewd.
My morals, putting it mildly, were lax.
My life was succinctly un-Christlike- I even
served a term in jail for late income tax.
I've watched these so-called Christian leaders,
the Swaggarts and Bakkers and such on TV;
Fat and rich and greedy and lewd,
succinctly un-Christlike, just like me.
But that's their plight and this is mine.
Did I save six billion? Not close to that many.
Now here at the end I'm asking myself
if indeed I ever saved any.
What about peace, did I bring it to Earth?
I tried, in my way, but I never got far.
I can hear the guns blasting, now as we speak
in Mosul and Gaza and Kandahar.
It's absurd, after all, why would You come
to a rocky South Korean hill
and ordain a fat boy, a recent Confucian,
to carry forth Your Almighty Will?
Now I'm dying, Lord Jesus, slipping away,
my organs are, one by one, shutting down.
Was I never a Messiah, the Grandson of God?
Was I ever anything more than a clown?

HIBERNIAN INDIGNATION

We Irish are the victims of calumnious connotations,
and speaking for myself, I disdain the implications
of the freighted Gaelic words like *finagle* and *banshee*
that define us as a rowdy crowd of *hooligans*- there, you
    see?
What do you call a Bangladeshi who trashes up the joint?
A Bangladeshi *hooligan.* I think you see my point.
I don't care to be defined by those libelous indicators;
I deny the allegations and resent the alligators.
I've never seen a *donnybrook* nor mixed a *Mickey Finn,*
haven't had a *whiskey* since when pompadours were in,
never wielded a *shillelagh,* though I was somewhat a *brat.*
Dishing out *malarkey*? Well yes, a bit of that.
What about *shenanigans*? One or two, no doubt,
but with just a bit of *blarney* I could *wheedle* my way out.

111

ONE HUSBAND'S VIEW ON CHRISTMAS WRAPPING

Helen wraps almost all of our presents:
artistry on display.
Every gift is a joy to behold,
together, a glistening array.
The only gifts she doesn't wrap
are those I buy for her.
But even if I bought her gold
and frankincense and myrrh,
they'd lie there in an artless pile,
bland in hue and shape,
each one wrapped in Wal-Mart paper,
fastened with Scotch Tape.
Here is how I wrap a gift:
What counts is what's inside it.
My job is not to gussy it up,
my job is just to hide it.

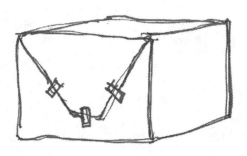

BYGONES

The hiker hitching a ride
has become exceedingly rare.
Beer can openers, skate keys?
Maybe at an antiques fair.

Blackboards, whiteout, phone booths,
the boombox and the fax,
Polaroid and Super 8,
gone the way of sealing wax.

Bookstores are fading fast,
replaced by Amazon,
and except in the state of Jersey,
gas attendants are gone.

The handkerchief we carried,
the stamps we used to lick,
the bankbook and the girdle
have joined the pogo stick

on the scrapheap of obsolescence,
along with the hotel key,
and on very rare occasions,
I fear, friends, even me.

GEEZER RESCUED FROM SUSPECTED DEMENTIA BY SMALL DOG

He is on the sofa, little Dinty by his side.
He ponders aloud:
    Upstairs, no, I looked.
    The kitchen, no, I looked.
    The table where I usually leave them,
    no, I looked twice.
    Home Depot.
    I took them to Home Depot to sign the Visa.
    I didn't use the Visa.
    A paint brush, $3.99 cash.
    A brush from the bottom bin, I leaned over.
    Out of my pocket onto the floor,
    mashed a minute later by a cart full of sheetrock.
    Maybe not. Maybe the car.
    Between the seats, like last time.
    Down between the
He feels eyes on him from the doorway, he looks down.
    seats, right, Dinty?

HOLIDAY MOTORING IN THE THIRTIES

Let's take a ride up the Hudson. Which side? The west,
in our new Hudson Terraplane; this will be its road test.
Up Broadway we go and across the new bridge, you and
    me,
onto 9W, which begins its career at Fort Lee.
Let's go for a leisurely lunch and a stroll in Tenafly
on this, the hottest-on-record Fourth of July.
The road is bendy, with non-stop traffic lights.
We came to sight-see, so let's see some of the sights.
Billboards, cows, an occasional hillside grave,
Nehi, Sweet Orr, Tydol-Veedol, Burma Shave.
There's a Ford hissing steam, its engine ticking down.
On a day like today they never should have left town.
The next Esso station is just three miles away;
one quart of water would suffice to save the day.
Water? How about wee-wee? To the radiator it's all the
    same.
With a Dad and three sons, a bottle and careful aim
the radiator cools, the car starts, to standing applause.
(What man over 70 has never peed a pint for the cause?)
They pull in at Esso, radiator whistling away.
It's a station-to-station adventure on a day like today.
The pump is manual, powered by hand with a crank.
The gas, on its way up and down and into your tank,
passes through what looks like a fishbowl up on the pump's
    top.
Gallon by gallon it gurgles, down to blip! the last drop.
Esso is amber, Richfield and Texaco too.
Only Sunoco, as it proudly proclaims, is blue.

A Reo on a jack, annoying but nothing dire;
if you know how to drive then you know how to change a
    tire.
Next day patch the tube, blow it up with a bicycle pump.
It's good until the next nail or abyssmal bump.
At times dogs and children, unaccustomed to automobiling,
can be seen relieving that God-awful nauseous feeling.
We open our windows to let in some cooler air;
wafting upon it is all that redolence out there;
cornfields, cowflops, roadkill, skunks and tar,
and the noisome exhausts of each passing truck and car.
There a smashed-up DeSoto, against a tree on the grass;
the sheen of blood, the glint of shattered glass.
What happened? A blowout? Maybe a wheel came off, or,
could it be when he stepped down, the brake pedal hit the
    floor?
It's hazardous, even perilous, this thirties automobiling,
all for that happy-motoring, king-of-the-road feeling.
Our Hudson is glorious, aromatically new-car now,
but it will dilapidate and die when the mileage hits fifty
    thou.
But, on the bright side, here's downtown Tenafly.
So, lunch and a stroll, my sweet wife, you and I?

MISSING, WITHOUT A TRACE

Wink Martindale, Jamie Farr,
Cyndi Lauper, Graham Kerr,
Macaulay Culkin, the Smothers Brothers,
Meatloaf, Fabian, Sally Struthers,
Arlo Guthrie, Huey Lewis, Katherine Harris, Joey Dee,
Piper Laurie, Micky Dolenz, Kasey Kasem, where can they
    be?
Frankie Avalon, Julius LaRosa, Little Richard, Al D'Amato,
Sister Souljah, Eddie Fisher, Edwin Meese, where have they
    got to?
Trini Lopez, Dennis Franz, Frank Gifford, Dave Barry,
Jack Kemp, Tom Hulce, Diana Dors, Debbie Harry,
PeeWee Herman, Janet Reno, Roger Clemens, James Arness,
Sammy Sosa, Soupy Sales, up and left, left no address.
Gary Burghoff, Robert Culp, Monica Lewinsky, Kato
    Kaelin,
and one of these days, please God, Sarah Palin.

POLITICALLY CORRECT

In a men's room it's P.C.
to leave the seat up après-pee.

A LOSS OF RESPECT

I was taught to respect my elders;
I've always kept that in mind.
It's only that as I grow older,
they're getting harder to find.

TO MY PUPPY ON A FEBRUARY DAY

Somewhere inside that little walnut brain
you accept your outside world as pallid,
the ground often white, sometimes slippery, always cold.
You cavort about, nuzzling snow, chasing squirrels.
You know that when you go to the door to come in,
it will open to a warm floor, squeaky toys, tasty treats,
a comfy bed, comfier laps.
And you sleep, four in the air.
But one day soon, little friend,
not very soon but soon,
that door will open out to a grassy lawn,
purple lilacs, chirpy wrens.
You'll roll in your clover,
patrol your green acres,
chase away deer and Canada geese,
and trot home feisty, full of terrier pluck.

VERMINOPHOBICS REJOICE!
A solution at last!

There's a type of woman in Brooklyn and Queens
who, fearful of germinating germs on my jeans,
as soon as I leave vacuums and cleans
the chair on which I sat.
She'll be ready for me next time I call
with plastic seat covers wall to wall,
on sofas, recliners, easy chairs all,
inviolable by me or the cat.
Madam, if I may, allow me to mention
my very latest ingenious invention.
It is guaranteed to assuage your tension
when folks drop in for a chat.
You open the door, say "Hello, my dear friends"
while over their heads a dispenser impends
and a dry cleaner's plastic wrap descends
and sanitizes each, whereat,
you welcome them in, a smile on your face,
the poster girl of cordial grace.
With the wave of a hand you say "Sit anyplace."
Comes in slim, medium and fat.

HUNTERDON COUNTY, NEW JERSEY

We have no tsunamis, no smog or monsoons,
no forest fires, oil spills, typhoons,
no riots, tidal waves, poisonous snakes,
no mine accidents, gang wars or quakes,
no terrorists, no tornadoes,
no pirates, no volcanos.

We have almost no heatwaves, deep freezes, blackouts,
blizzards, hurricanes, floods or droughts.

We have too many gnats and geese and Republicans
to suit me,
but on balance, a good place to be.

AN URGENT MESSAGE TO JOURNALISM MAJORS

While they're still printing newspapers,
check and see who's looking for what.
There are several industries offering work
and one most emphatically not.
Wanted: accountants, bartenders and maids,
teachers, mechanics, dentists and aides,
bookkeepers, nurses, drivers of trucks,
programmers aplenty, earning good bucks.
Big money awaits every cyberspace whiz
and expert in IT, whatever that is.
But journalists wanted? Nary a one.
Zero, not even copyboys, none.
So make that switch quickly now,
while there's still time.
None of the above, you say, turns you on?
Mmm, well then, what about crime?

IMPORTANT THINGS WE'VE LEARNED FROM THE MOVIES

When the cops pull up there's always a place to park,
women must wear frilly nighties, investigating sounds in
    the dark,
the ventilation duct is a perfect place to hide,
any lock can be picked, unless there's a child trapped
    inside,
555 are the opening numbers of every telephone,
all foreigners speak English when they're alone,
medieval peasants had perfect teeth in their head,
out of every grocery bag sticks a loaf of French bread,
investigators all must go to watch lewd women strip,
the bill you pull to pay the cab is right, including tip,
anyone can land a plane, the tower will talk you down,
Parisians all can see their Tower, from every window in
    town,
yank that steering wheel left and right when your car is
    being chased,the sheets come up to her armpits but only
    up to his waist,
only a suspended detective can solve a murder case
and a single match will light a room the size of outer
    space.

WINDBREAKERS II

The latest from medical science,
just released today:

Tina Fey and Joel McCrea,
I.M. Pei, Maurice Chevalier,
Doris Day and Rachel Ray,
Mel Tormé and Henry Clay,
Nanette Fabray and Murray the K,
Beyoncé, John LeCarré,
Josephine Tey and Peter Roget,
Ken Lay and Joel Grey,
Claude Monet and Martha Raye,
Ron Cey and Mary Kay,
Fay Wray and Doctor J,
LL Cool J and Tom DeLay,

each and every one farts or farted
14 times a day.

THE WASHINGTON REDSKINS: IS THE NAME OFFENSIVE?

"Certainly not," says Sherman Alexie,
Native American writer of note,
"with one proviso, small but vital:
(This is, I believe, an accurate quote.)
Other teams in the league would include
the Brooklyn Kikes and the Boston Micks,
the Dallas Coons, the Jersey Wops,
the Cleveland Krauts and the L.A. Spicks.
Now that sounds eminently fair to me.
If they don't mind, why should we?"

COPACABANA

Billy Collins wrote
that there's always a song playing in his head,
rarely one of his choosing,
"More Than a Woman" at composition time.
I wondered if this is a universal affliction,
so I asked three people, all yesses;
with Billy, my wife and me,
that's six of six, so maybe.
Mine is a thousand-disc Wurlitzer,
seventy years of melodies,
Mozart to Manilow, fight songs and commercials.
Any whim will set one spinning,
though it's often just a shard:
"We are three caballeros, three gay caballeros,
da dum dada dum dada dumdum..."
Again and again...
I can't pull the plug but I can push a button;
"Rag Mop" can be willed over to Joplin or Brel.
But left to its own playlist,
my box, like his, selects the droopiest of ditties.
It is my abiding fear that in those final moments,
the ultimate canticle in my head,
just as the sound cuts off,
will be, not a glorious oratorio, but
"...and they went upon their abbadabba honeym